Bear Coloring Book

Volume 2

30 Hand Drawn, Doodle and Folk Art Style Teddy Bear Themed Adult Coloring Pages

ISBN-13: 978-1539123781
ISBN-10: 1539123782

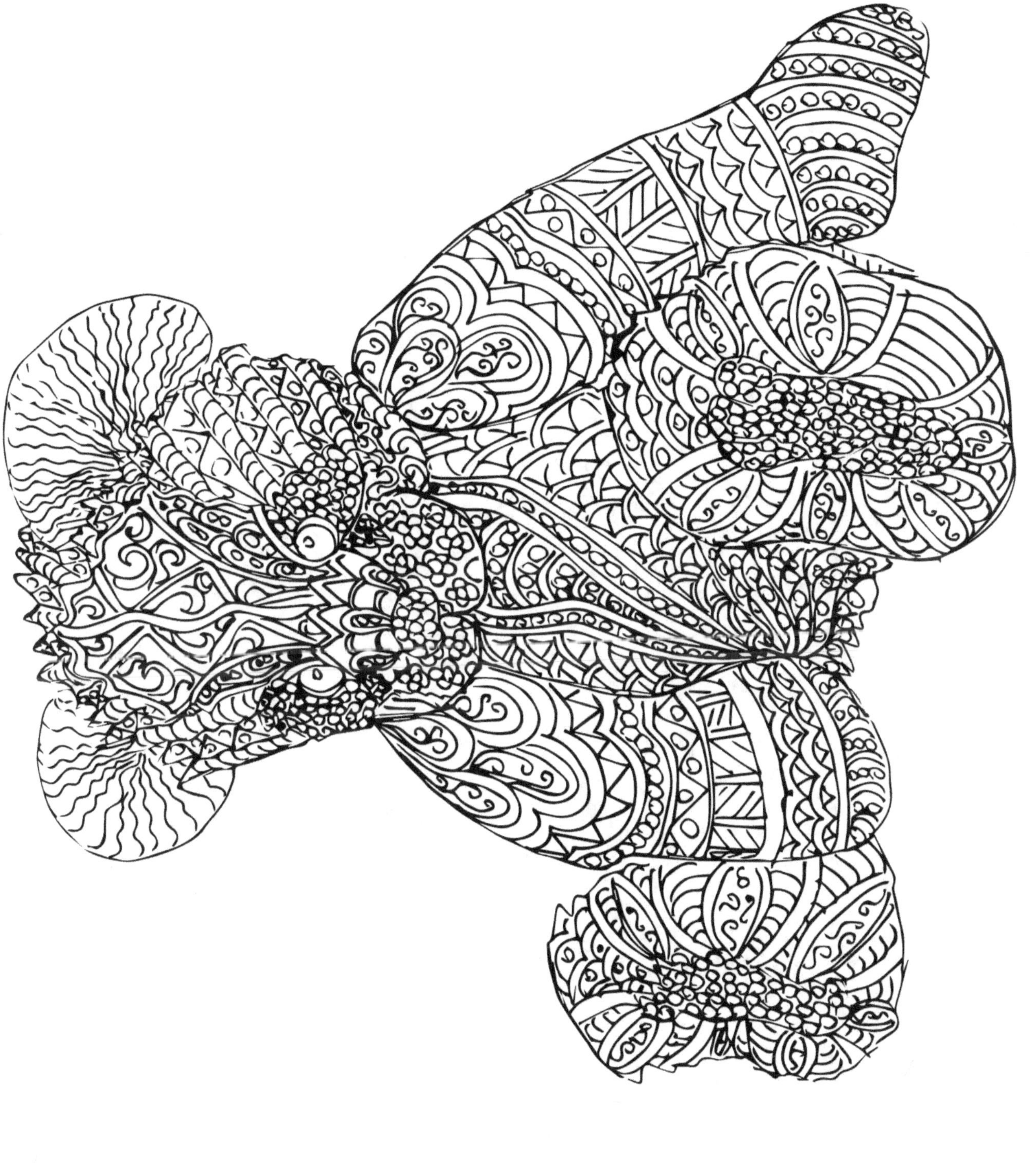

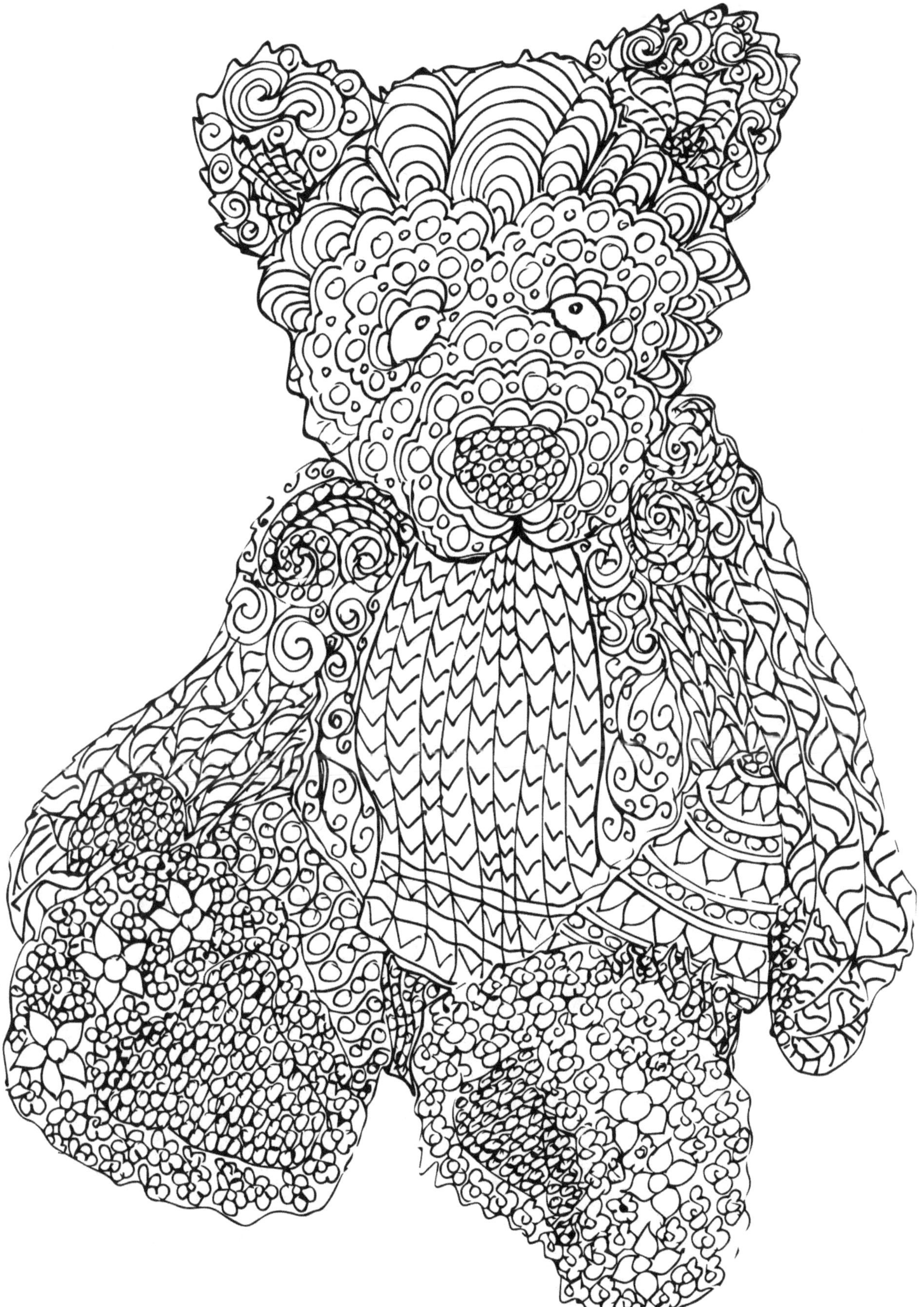

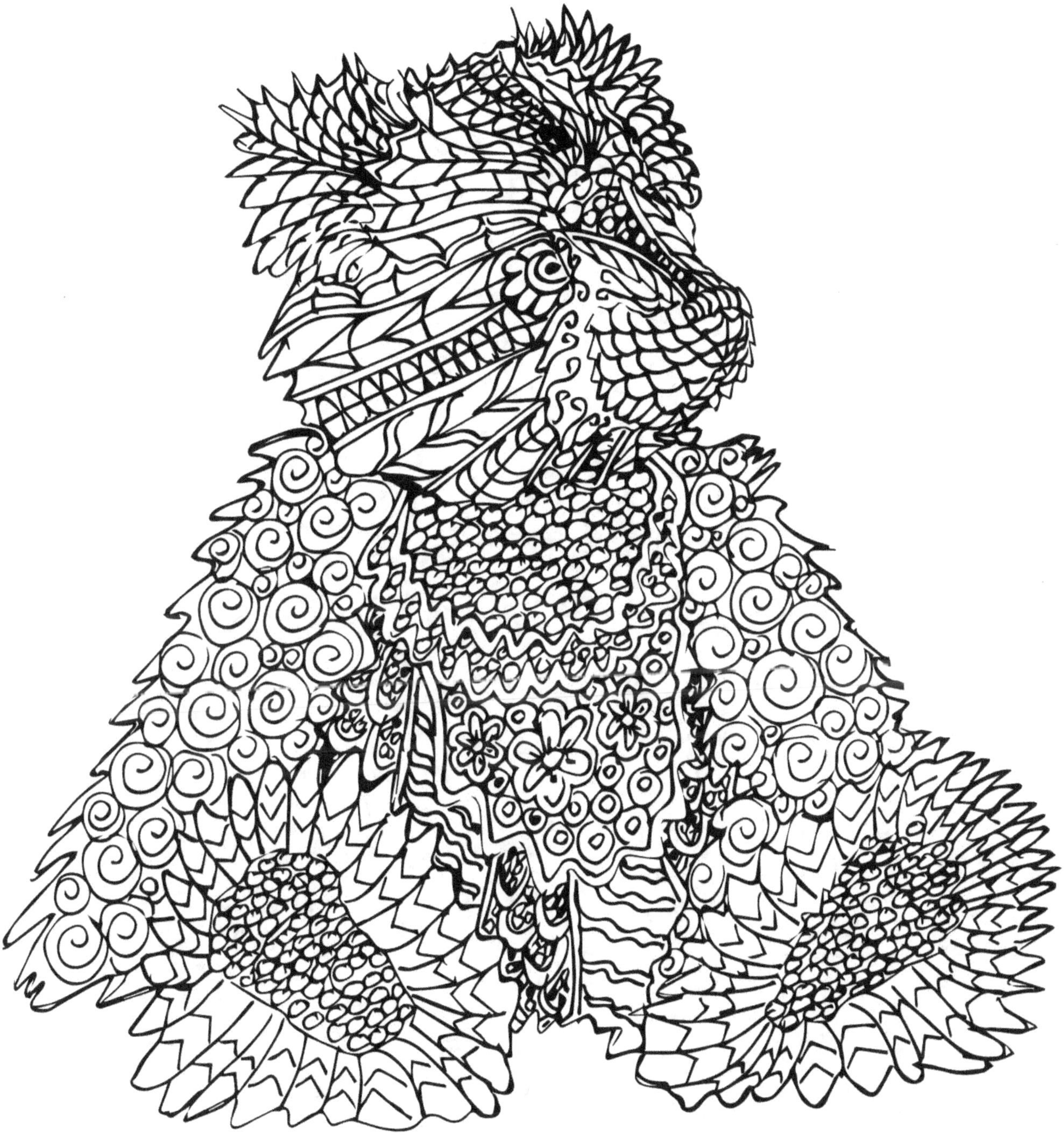

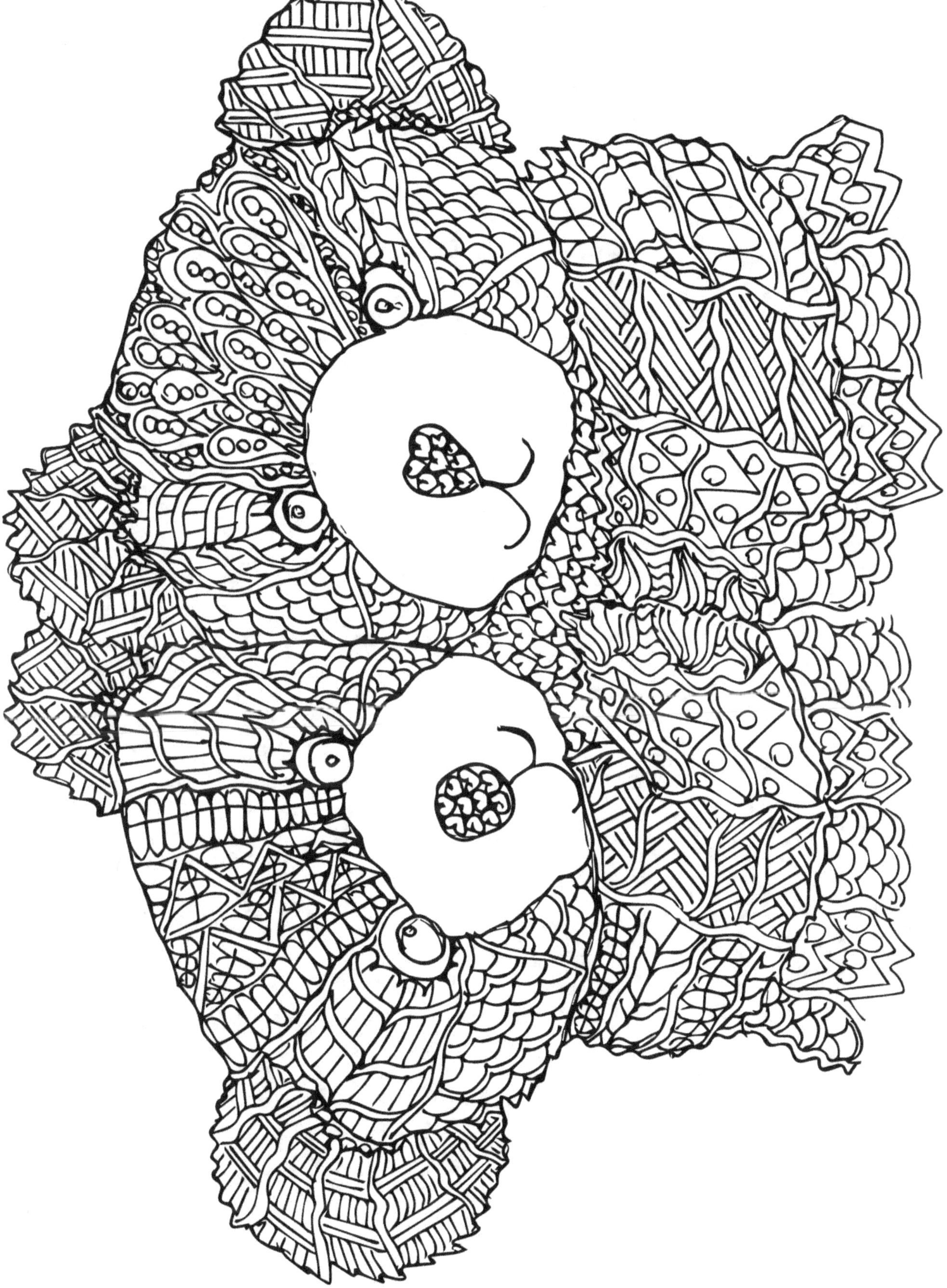

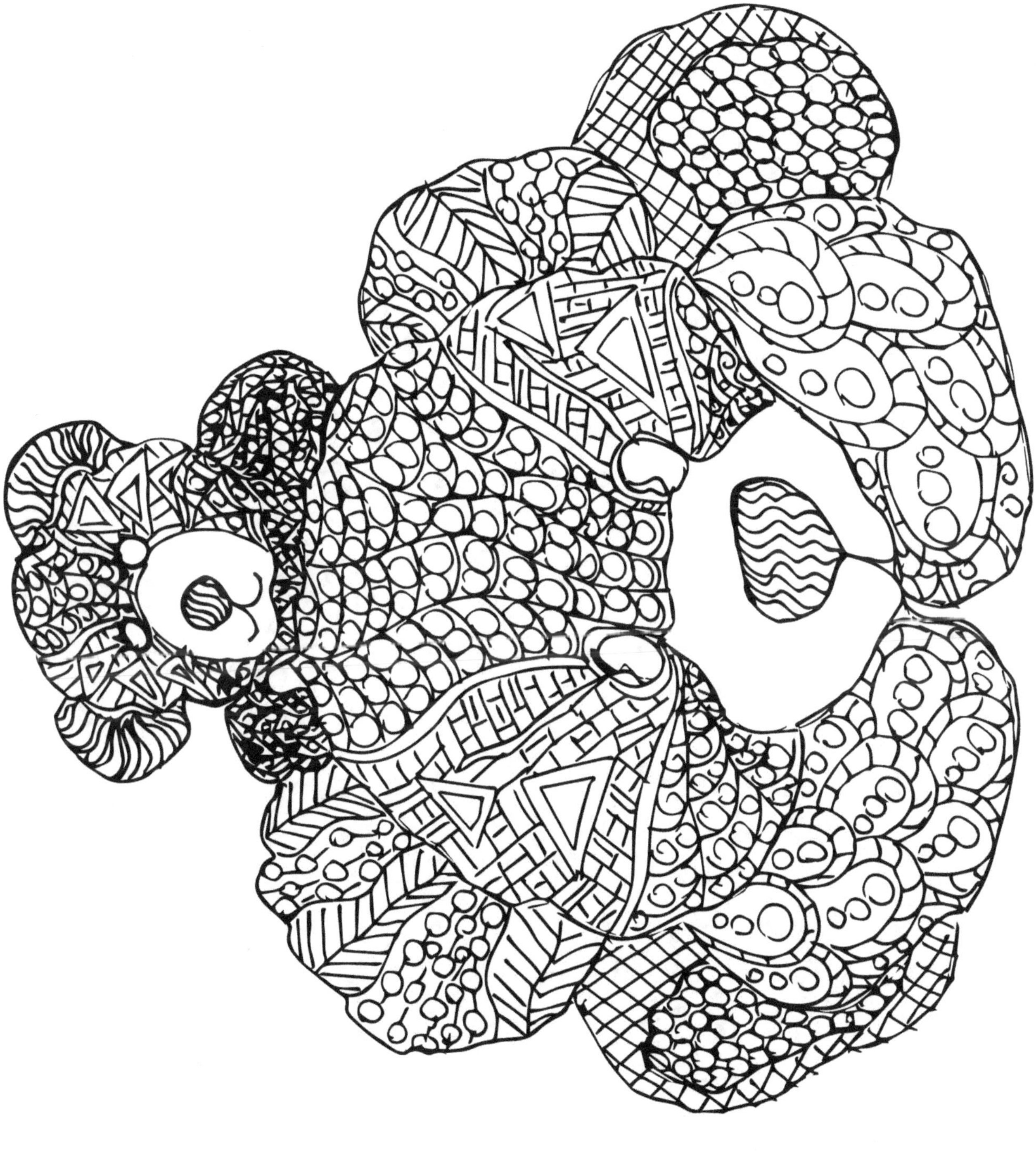

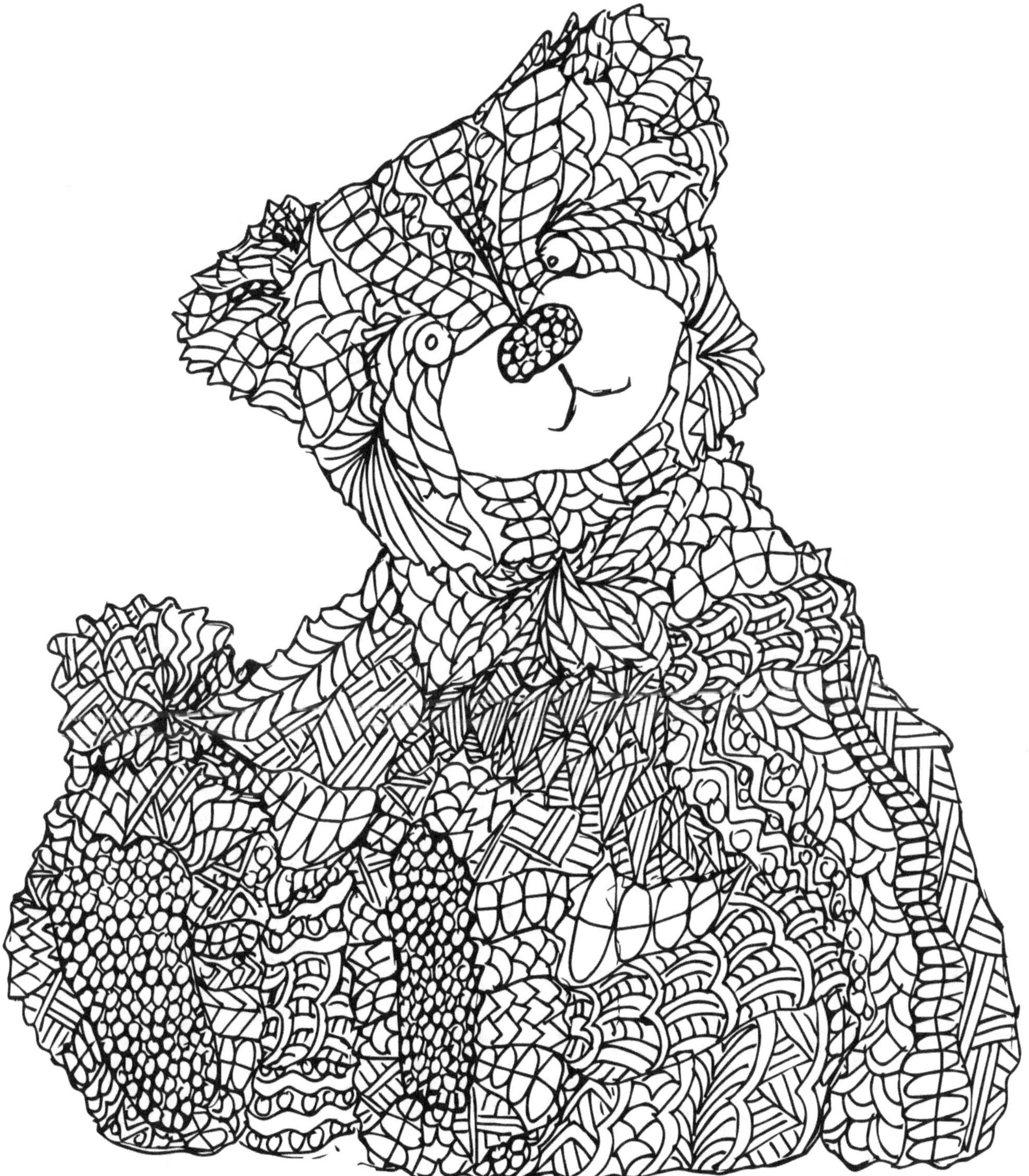

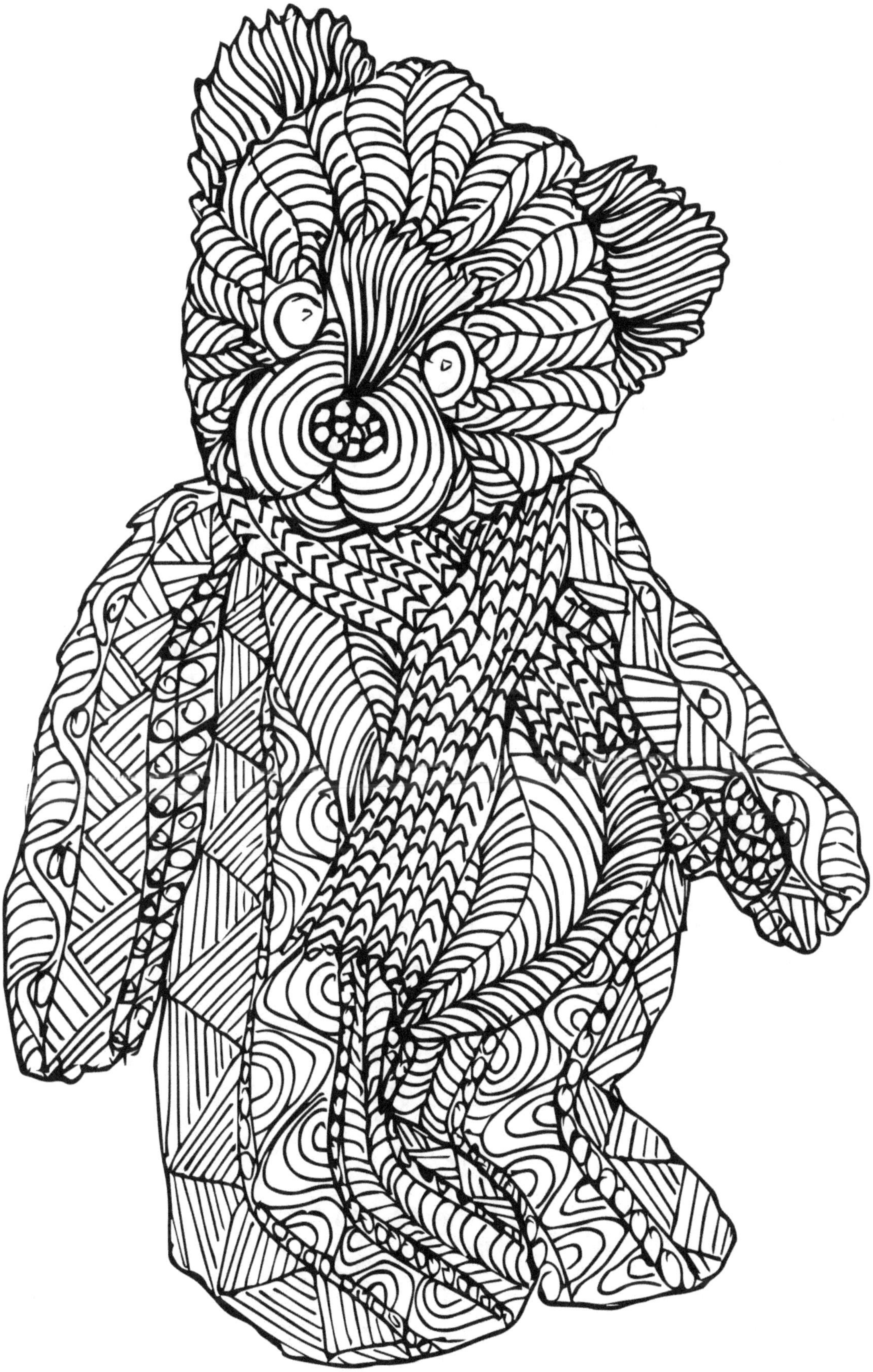

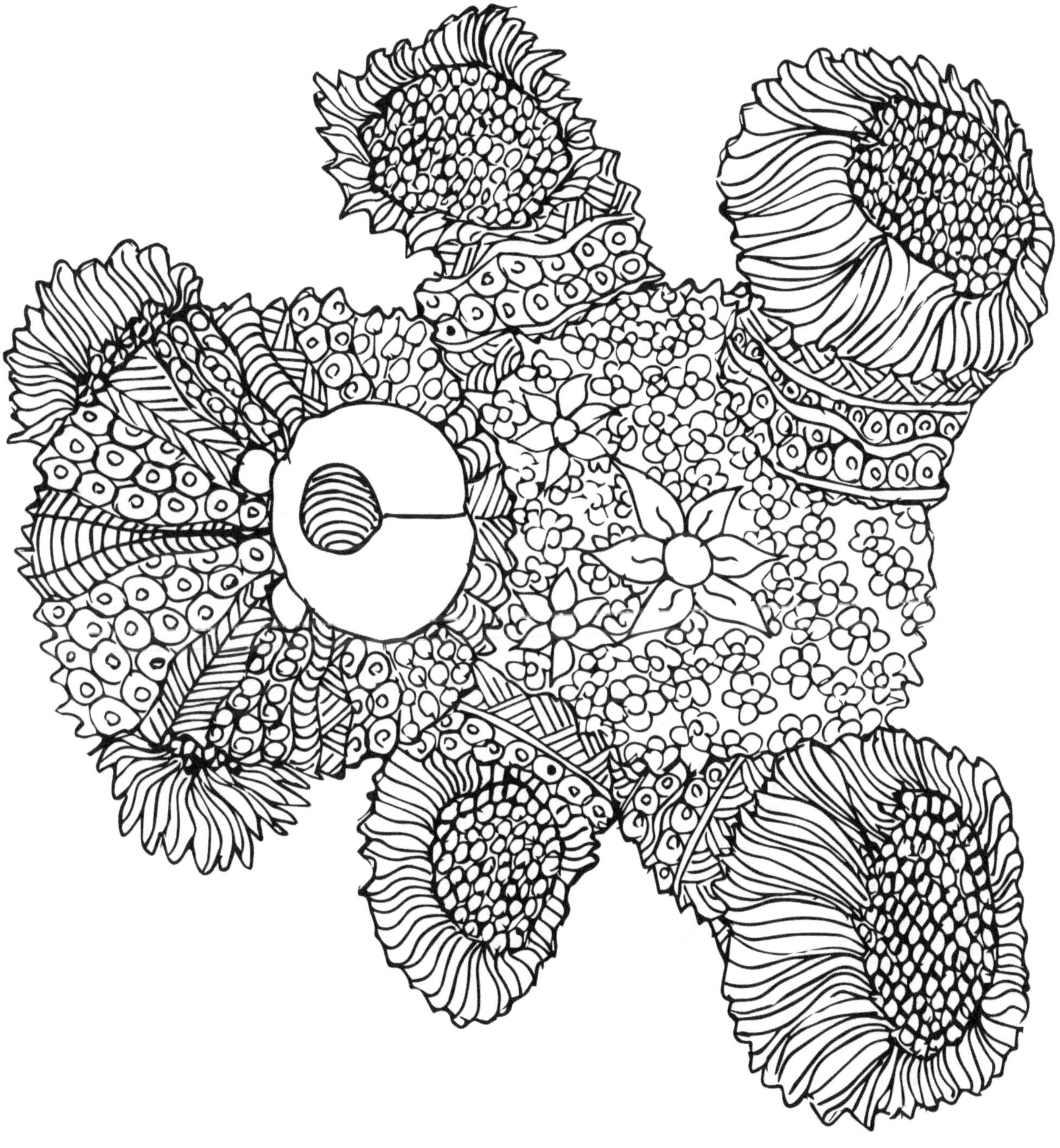

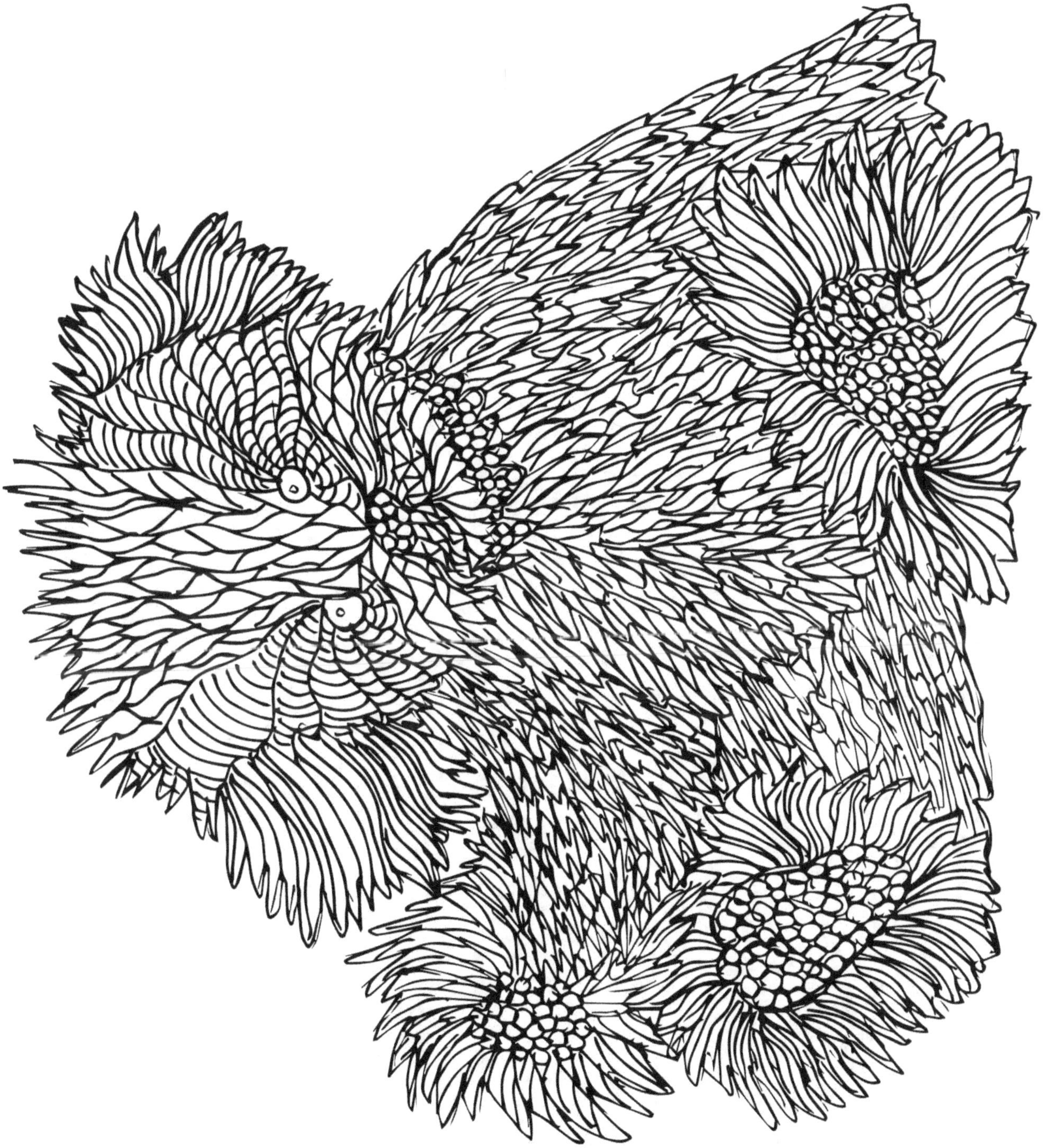

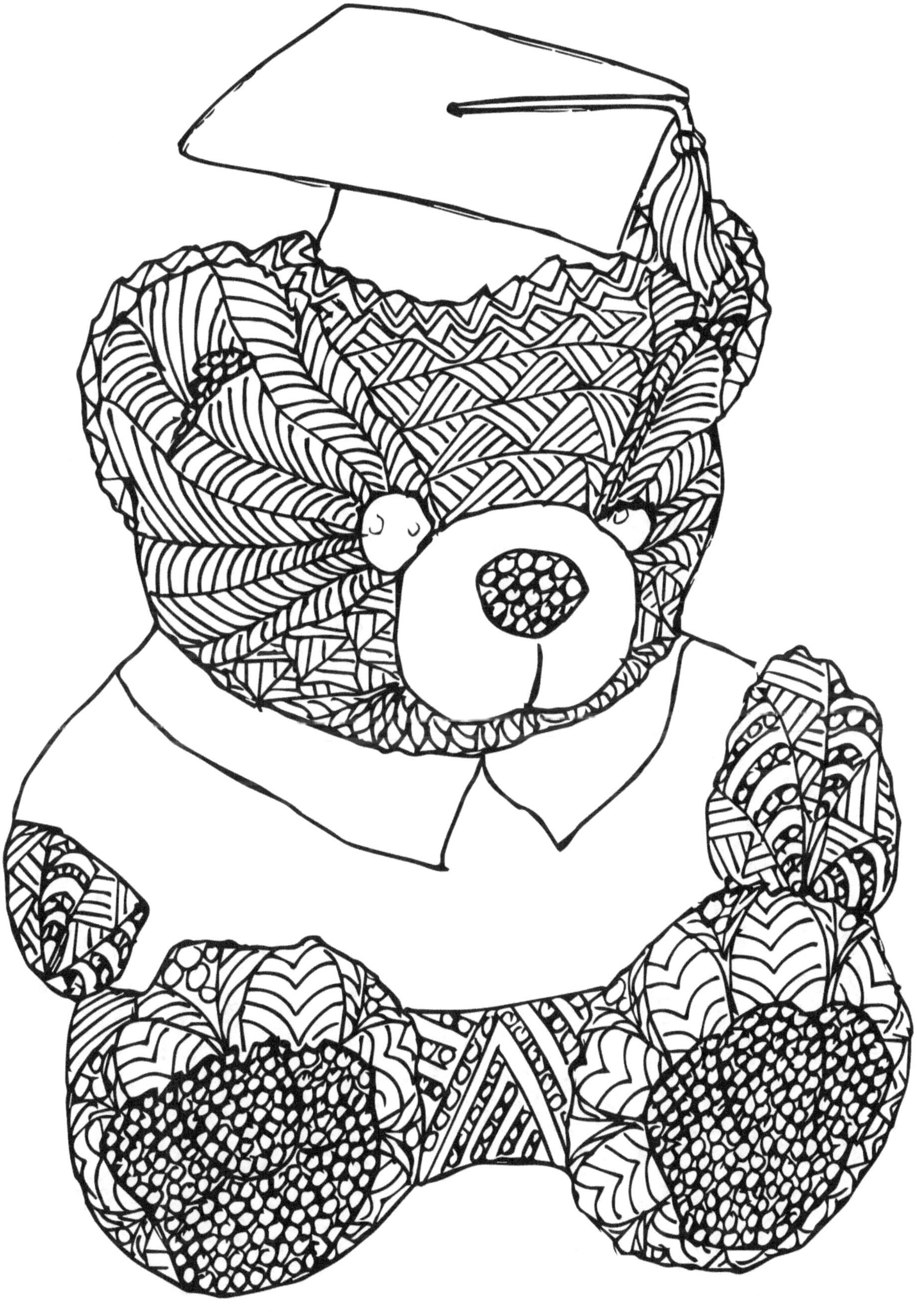

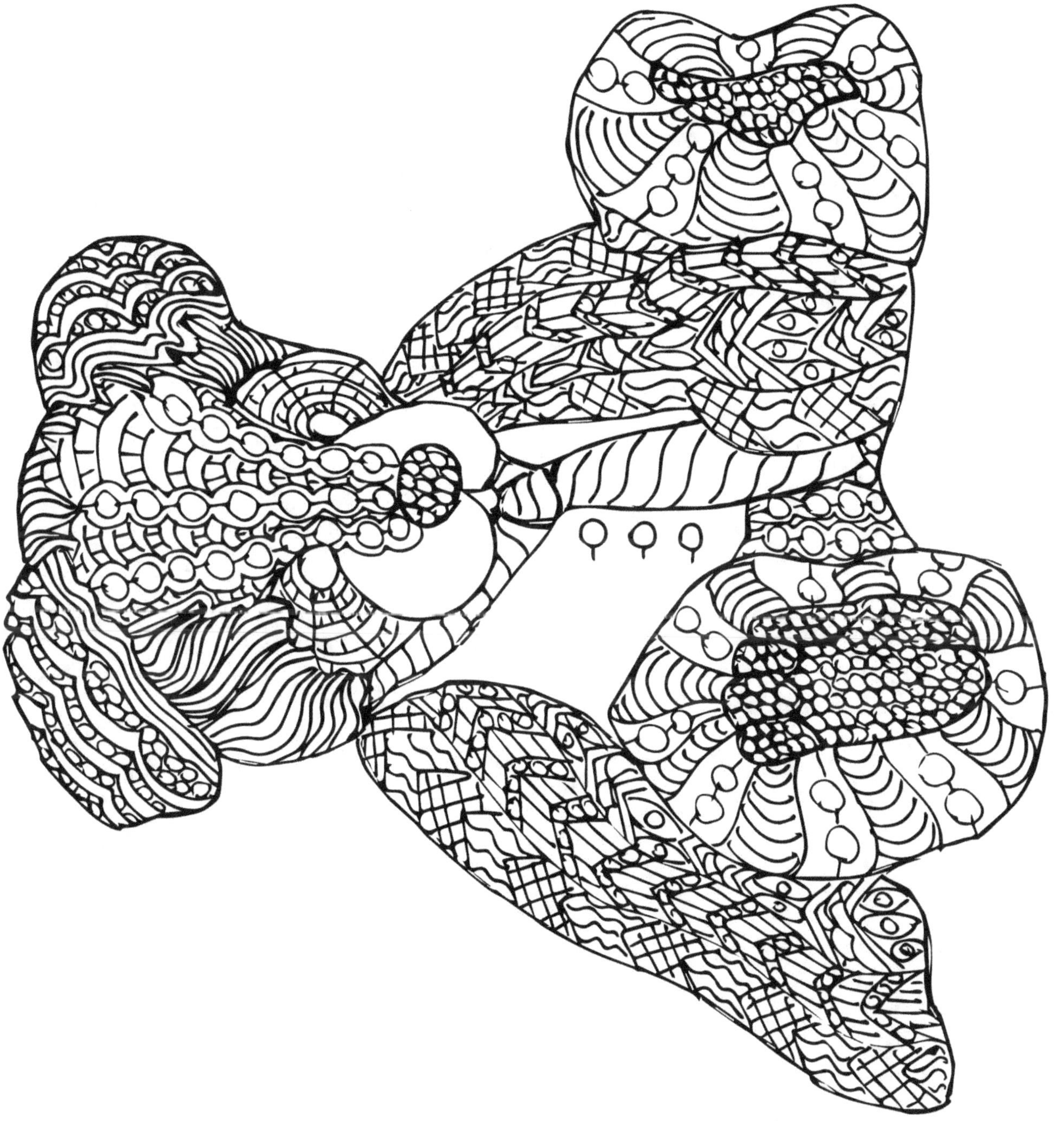

www.ingramcontent.com/pod-product-compliance
Lightning Source LLC
Chambersburg PA
CBHW081858280526
45789CB00007B/2757